S0-AXW-705

THE BEST COOKIN' IN THE COUNTRY

THE BEST COOKIN' IN THE COUNTRY

Compiled by Tom Wiecks

Illustrations by Tom Bowman
Cover Illustration by Newman Myrah

Barleycorn Books

Copyright © 1979 by Tom Wiecks
All rights reserved

Published by Barleycorn Books
290 SW Tualatin Loop
West Linn, Oregon 97068

International Standard Book Number 0-935566-00-7
Library of Congress Catalog Number 79-91262

Designed by Tom Wiecks
Typesetting by SeTyp
Printed by Times Litho

Manufactured in the United States of America

To Carolyn, who did everything else
while I did this

FOREWORD

There I was doing my Sunday night show on KWJJ in Portland. My stomach was growling. It always growled on Sunday nights because it never got fed until around 1 am. I was afraid if I ate sooner I'd end up taking a nap in the middle of the show, and I figured it was better for my stomach to growl at me than the station manager.

Anyway, since all I was thinking about was food and which artists to play next, somehow the two got together in my head and this book started. Before long, I was writing letters to most of Nashville and here we are.

But I ended up learning a whole lot more in the course of things than how to make pumpkin bread, cucumber salad and three kinds of chili. I also learned a few things about the folks behind all those country records.

For one thing, you know that myth about the kid who maybe grows up kind of poor, learns to pick, makes a hit record and becomes a big star with all the glitter and everything, but still stays pretty much the same person he/she always was? Well, as far as I can see, it's true.

I imagine most of the stars represented here could dine nightly on lobster tails and caviar if they wanted to. But it seems they don't want to. Most of the recipes we received — all of them favorites of the contributing artists — are for pretty simple, downhome kind of dishes. They're the kind of everyday fare everyday people eat.

And that makes me feel good since country music is supposed to be sort of a voice for us common folks. If "you are what you eat" like they say, it's probably also true that "you eat what you are."

Then there's the somewhat surprising fact that these stars would answer a letter from someone they'd never heard of in the first place (in West Linn, Oregon, no less). And not only answer, but in many cases, go to some trouble in doing so.

One dropped everything while she was on tour and, lacking stationery, scribbled out a recipe on the back of my letter and sent it back to me.

One telephoned me personally to pass along a favorite pie recipe. My letter had gotten buried in a pile of things, and he wanted to make sure I hadn't been inconvienced by the delay!

And many answered with handwritten notes a couple of pages long wishing us luck with the book. They read like letters from old friends, which come to think of it is exactly what they were, though we'd never met.

So I've been pretty impressed with these people as people. Somehow I doubt that rock stars or jazz stars or whatever would be as generous as a group. And that goes for the folks who represent these stars at the various talent agencies, too. We couldn't have put all these recipes together without their help and it's appreciated.

While I'm at it, I should thank my friends the kitchen testers who kneaded dough, chopped parsley and squeezed lemons in the interest of accuracy and good eating. They are J.B. and Carol Williams, Rob and Gail Reynolds, John and Ann Cowger, Jack and Ann Messick, and I better not forget my good wife Carolyn. Their assistance was not always easy to render. Have you ever tried to go out and buy file' gumbo in Oregon?

Finally, let me give special thanks to Newman Myrah who did the drawing on the cover of Johnny Cash, Charlie Rich, Bill Anderson, Glen Campbell, Anne Murray and Tom T. Hall. Besides being a country music fan and a heck of a nice guy, Newm is one of the most widely acclaimed Western artists (the kind who paints) in the country, and I sure appreciate his help.

So that's it. In the Table of Contents that follows, you'll find 49 favorite dishes from 49 of the world's favorite country stars, and I hope you enjoy them all. In the back, you'll find an index which lists the recipes by category.

At one time the book also had an appendix, but just before press time it became inflamed and had to be removed.

TABLE OF CONTENTS

ROY ACUFF'S VEGETABLE BEEF SOUP

1 lb. lean beef, cubed
About 3 quarts of cold water
1 tblsp. salt
Pepper to taste
2 stalks celery
½ cup green pepper, cubed
1 onion, minced
1 bay leaf

1 can tomatoes
1 cup each of diced potatoes,
    carrots, cabbage, green beans
    and turnips
½ cup dried Great Northern beans
¼ cup each of rice, barley and
    split peas

"**B**rown the cubed beef in a couple tablespoons of shortening. Then add the other ingredients and bring everything to a boil.

"Cook on low heat for about two and a half or three hours. If it turns out too thick, just add more water. This recipe serves about 12."

REX ALLEN, JR'S. CHEESE GRITS

4 cups boiling water
1 tsp. salt
1 cup instant grits
½ cup butter

8 oz. cheddar cheese
Garlic to taste
2 or 3 eggs
1 cup milk

"Salt the water, bring it to a boil and slowly stir in the grits. Cook for three minutes, stirring constantly.

"Then remove from heat and stir in the butter, cheese and garlic.

"Break the eggs into a cup. Then mix the milk in with the eggs and add them to the grits mixture.

"Now, pour it all into a greased casserole and bake for an hour at 350 degrees."

BILL ANDERSON'S BEEF STEW

3 lb. sirloin tip roast
  (cut in bite size pieces)
6 tblsp. shortening
2 medium onions, chopped
5 cups water
1½ cup red cooking wine
2 beef bouillon cubes
2 tblsp. minced garlic
A few sprigs of parsley
1 bay leaf

A dash of thyme
1½ tsp. salt
¼ tsp. pepper
10 medium potatoes
10 medium carrots
10 small white onions
2 medium green peppers
2 medium tomatoes,
  cut in chunks

"**H**eat the shortening in a large heavy skillet or pot, add the meat and cook until it's brown. Then remove the meat and brown the onions until they're limp.

"Return the meat to the skillet and add the water, wine, bouillon cubes, garlic, parsley, bay leaf, thyme, salt and pepper. Bring it all to a boil. Then reduce the heat, cover and cook slowly for one and a half hours.

"Next, peel the potatoes and carrots and cut them in pieces. Add them and the white onions to the skillet or pot and cook gently for one hour, or until tender. Add the peppers and tomatoes about 20 minutes before the end of the cooking time.

"You can thicken the gravy with a little flour if you like. Then serve it up for about six to eight stew eaters."

CHET ATKINS' BLACK EYED PEAS

2 cups black eyed peas
¼ lb. bacon
   (with a streak of lean)

1 tsp. salt, or to taste

"Wash the peas thoroughly in cold water. Then place in a heavy sauce pan, cover completely with cold water and let them soak overnight.

"In the morning you may either drain the water and cook the peas in fresh water, or cook them in the water in which they were soaked. I've tried both ways and either way is good. You might lose some of the vitamins if you drain.

"Place the heavy sauce pan on your burner with plenty of water to cover the peas — I'd say about a half inch over the top of them. Add the bacon sliced to the rind in half-inch slices and the salt. A dash or two of black pepper is good also.

"Bring to a boil and simmer for two hours. Then taste to see if there's enough salt. If not, add more to taste.

"If the peas have too much soup for your liking, remove the cover and simmer some more. If you prefer more soup, add more water and simmer a little longer."

HOYT AXTON'S MEXICO CITY SPECIAL

½ pint cognac (or brandy)
½ stick of butter

½ lb. of hamburger made
into patties
Salt and pepper to taste

"I learned this when I was doing a movie down in Mexico, so I call it the Mexico City Special.

"First, you soak the hamburger in the cognac for a while. What the hamburger doesn't soak up, you can later. No sense in wasting it.

"Simmer the hamburger patties in the butter for about 22 minutes, turning every five minutes. Salt and pepper them to your taste.

"Then serve them with corn chips or potato chips, plus one carrot, one stick of celery, one slice of tomato and one piece of parsley. For me, the vegetation is just for decoration, not to eat.

"Use a 16 oz. glass of non-fat milk with 4 ice cubes as your beverage. Plus, of course, the cognac."

BOBBY BARE'S SOUTHERN GREEN BEANS

2 lbs. fresh pole beans
6 cups water
½ lb. smoked hog jowl

¼ cup sliced onion
1 tsp. paprika
Salt to taste

"First, prepare the beans by snapping, stringing and washing them thoroughly. When that's done, put the beans and all the other ingredients in a large pot and boil it all for at least 20 minutes.

"Then reduce the heat to a medium temperature and continue to cook until there's a very small amount of water in the bottom of the pan. With these beans, the slower they cook the better they'll taste.

"The next step is to sit down and enjoy them with cornbread and buttermilk."

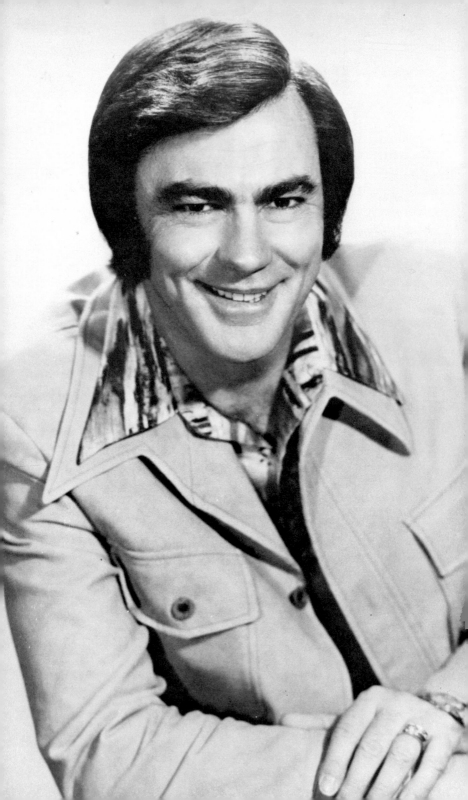

JIM ED BROWN'S FRUIT SALAD

1 large can fruit cocktail
1 cup miniature marshmallows
1 pint strawberries, sliced

3 bananas, sliced
1 cup heavy whipping cream
½ cup chopped walnuts

"This one's real simple. You just whip the cream until it's stiff, fold in the fruit, nuts and marshmallows, and chill it an hour before you serve it.

"Simply delicious."

GLEN CAMPBELL'S CHORIZO SOUP

½ lb. dried garbanzo beans or
   chick peas
1 lb. chorizo sausages (or pepperoni)
   cut in ½" slices
1 cup chopped onion
1 cup chopped green pepper
½ cup chopped celery
3 cloves garlic, crushed
3 tblsp. chili powder

1 16 oz. can stewed tomatoes
½ cup raw long-grained white rice
2 envelopes instant beef broth
   (or 2 beef bouillon cubes)
1 tblsp. salt
1 tsp. cumin seed
½ tsp. black pepper
6 cups water

"**S**tart off by soaking the garbanzo beans in water overnight in a covered bowl. The next day, drain them and set them aside while you saute the chorizo slices in a dutch oven or a big heavy kettle.

"Once the chorizo is evenly browned, remove it with a slotted spoon and set it aside, too. But leave the sausage fat in the bottom of the dutch oven. That's what you saute the onion, green pepper, celery and garlic in for about seven to ten minutes, or until the onion's all golden.

"Then you stir in the chili powder and let it cook for a minute. Next, add the stewed tomatoes, rice, instant beef broth, salt, cumin seed, pepper and six cups of water, and stir everything until the beef broth is dissolved.

31

"Toss in the garbanzos and bring the soup to a boil. Then cover it, and let everything simmer for 45 minutes or until the garbanzos are nice and tender. The last thing you put in is the browned chorizo, letting the soup simmer another 15 minutes.

"Serve it in a deep casserole and if you like, top it off with some green onions sliced really thin. You'll have enough for about six soup eaters.

"By the way, this dish can also be served as a stew. Just leave out the half cup of raw rice and reduce the amount of water to four cups."

BILLY CARTER'S LEMON MERINGUE PIE

1 cup sugar
¼ cup cornstarch
½ tsp. salt
1/3 cup cold water
1-1/3 cup lemon juice

1 tsp. lemon rind
1/3 cup lemon juice
3 egg yolks, slightly beaten
2 tblsp. butter (or margarine)
1 9-inch baked pie shell

"Combine the sugar, cornstarch and salt in a saucepan, and blend in the cold water. Then add the hot water. Cook over medium heat stirring constantly for five to eight minutes, until it gets thick and clear.

"Remove the mixture from the heat to stir in the lemon rind and lemon juice. Then cook it for another two minutes.

"Next, take about a half cup of this hot mixture and blend it into the egg yolks in a bowl. Then return it all to the saucepan and cook for two more minutes, stirring constantly.

"Add the butter, cover the pan and let it cool to lukewarm. Once it has, pour it into a nine-inch pastry shell you've already baked and top it with meringue.

"Bake at 350 degrees for 10 to 12 minutes, then let it cool."

JOHNNY CARVER'S RED BEANS & RICE

1 package of dried red
  kidney beans
A pinch of baking soda
2 15 oz. cans of tomato sauce
2 cans of water (use tomato
  sauce cans)

2 smoked ham hocks or 4 or 5
  smoked link sausages
1 large onion, chopped
4 cloves garlic, minced
Dash of Tobasco sauce
Dash of Worcestershire sauce

"Soak the beans in water with a pinch of baking soda overnight. Then rinse them, put them back in the pot and toss in the rest of the ingredients.

"Cook it all slowly for about three or four hours, stirring occasionally. Then serve over rice and you're set."

JOHNNY CASH'S SOYA BREAD

7 cups stone ground whole
   wheat flour
1½ cups soya grits
1 cup 7-grain cereal
1 cup granola
½ cup chopped mixed nuts

1 cup honey
1 cup soybean oil
4 eggs
3 tblsp. dry yeast
6 cups warm water
Salt to taste

"**M**ix all the dry ingredients together. Then put the yeast in the warm water, and let it sit for five minutes.

"Slowly mix the dry ingredients into the yeast mixture. Next, combine the oil, eggs and honey with the yeast mixture. Then knead the dough for five minutes.

"Shape it into three loaves. Let them rise in a warm place for an hour. Then go ahead and bake them at 350 degrees for 45 minutes."

JUNE CARTER CASH'S SAUSAGE ROLLS

2 cups self-rising flour
¼ cup shortening

¾ cup buttermilk
1 or 2 lbs. ground sausage

"Mix the flour, shortening and buttermilk together and roll it out in a long roll. Then put the sausage between sheets of wax paper and roll it out the same length as your dough.

"Place the sausage on top of the dough. And just roll it up from the smallest end, like you would a jelly roll.

"Then put it in the freezer overnight. The next day, slice it and bake it at 350 to 400 degrees until it's lightly browned."

CONNIE CATO'S SQUASH CASSEROLE

3 medium squash, cooked
2 medium onions
1 can of water chestnuts, sliced
1 8 oz. carton sour cream

1 can of Cream of Chicken soup
1 package of Pepperidge Farm
   Herb Dressing
1 stick of margarine

"Melt the margarine, mix it into the dressing and put half of it into a casserole dish.

"Then mix the cooked squash with the onion, the chestnuts, the soup and the sour cream, and pour it all into the casserole.

"Put the rest of the dressing mix on top. Then bake it at 350 degrees for 30 to 40 minutes.

"This recipe's been handed down in my husband's family for years. Served with almost any meat, it's fit for a king."

JERRY CLOWER'S MISSISSIPPI CUCUMBER SALAD

5. medium cucumbers
1 cup vinegar
2 tblsp. water
1 tblsp. salad oil
1 tblsp. sugar
1 tsp. salt

½ tsp. pepper
1 large onion, coarsely
    chopped
1 tsp. dried parsley flakes
½ tsp. dill seeds

"Peel the cucumbers and slice 'em real thin. Then mix up the rest of the ingredients and pour it all over the cucumbers and onions.

"Let it marinate at least three hours in the refrigerator before serving.

"Bet it's gone before you can spell M-i-s-s-i-s-s-i-p-p-i."

HELEN CORNELIUS' LASAGNE ROMA

1 lb. ground beef
½ lb. pork sausage
1 clove garlic, minced
¾ cup chopped onions
15 oz. can tomato sauce
1 lb. can tomatoes
2 tblsp. chopped parsley
2 tsp. sugar

1 tsp. salt
¼ tsp. each of marjoram, thyme,
    oregano and basil
1½ cups cubed mozzarella cheese
1½ lbs. ricotta cheese
1 cup grated Parmesan cheese
8 oz. package lasagne noodles,
    cooked

"**S**tart off by browning the ground beef, pork sausage, garlic and onion in a big saucepan. Drain off all the fat. Then add the tomato sauce, tomatoes, parsley, sugar, salt and spices and simmer it all uncovered for about an hour, or until the consistency looks right to you.

"Next, heat your oven to 350 degrees and pour a half cup of the sauce into a baking pan. Then put in alternating layers of noodles, grated cheese, mozzarella, spoonfuls of riccota cheese and sauce until all the ingredients are used up. Make the top layer sauce and grated cheese and bake for one hour.

"I like to serve this with a tossed green salad, buttered Italian green beans and a fruit dessert of some kind. My family loves Italian cooking so much we should have been Italian!"

FLOYD CRAMER'S BUTTERMILK PIE

5 eggs
3 cups sugar
2 tblsp. cornstarch
1 cup buttermilk

1½ tsp. vanilla
1 cup butter
1 9 inch unbaked pie shell

"All you need to do is mix everything together and heat it up until it's warm. Then pour it into an unbaked pie shell.

"After about 35 or 40 minutes at 350 degrees, I think you'll see why I like this pie."

ROY DRUSKY'S CORN BREAD

2 cups self-rising corn meal
½ cup self-rising flour
½ cup sugar
1 package dry yeast

1 egg
3 tblsp. bacon grease
2 cups buttermilk

"**M**ix the dry ingredients together and sprinkle in the yeast. Then beat in the egg and buttermilk and add the bacon grease. Bake in a large loaf pan at 325 degrees for one hour.

"I like this recipe because it's a good old fashioned country bread. It's great warm, or sliced thick and fried in butter. You can serve it with any meal including breakfast if it's browned in butter."

NARVEL FELTS' LEMON ICEBOX PIE

1 can Eagle brand milk
2 egg yolks

1 cup fresh squeezed lemon juice
Vanilla wafers

"First, combine the Eagle brand milk and the egg yolks, and beat them by hand for about two hundred strokes.

"Then add the lemon juice and beat for another two hundred strokes.

"For the pie crust, line a pie pan with vanilla wafers on the bottom and the sides. Pour the filling in, then top the pie with vanilla wafer crumbs.

"Put the pie in the refrigerator and chill for two hours before serving."

DON GIBSON'S CHICKEN & PILAF

1 whole chicken, cut up
¼ lb. butter (one stick)
1 lb. fresh mushrooms
1½ cups white wine

Pilaf:
½ cup spaghetti in 1 inch pieces
1 cup rice
¼ cup butter (½ stick)
2 cups chicken broth

"**W**hile you melt a stick of butter, get your mushrooms nice and clean. Add the wine to the melted butter, then the mushrooms. Let them cook a bit, then pour everything over the chicken in a 13″ by 9″ by 2″ baking dish. Bake it for an hour at 350 degrees while you make the pilaf.

"The pilaf's real simple. You just brown the spaghetti in butter, then add the rice and the broth and bring it to a boil. Then you let it simmer another 35 minutes.

"Chances are, you'll like both these dishes by themselves. But wait'll you try them together."

JACK GREENE'S ZUCCHINI

4 tblsp. oil
2 large zucchini
1 small onion, chopped
¼ tsp. pepper
¼ tsp. salt

2 tblsp. (or more) grated
    Parmesan cheese
8 oz. can tomato sauce
3 slices processed
    Swiss cheese

"Cut the zucchini into quarter inch slices and saute in oil with the chopped onion for five minutes.

"Add the salt and pepper and Parmesan cheese, and toss lightly. Then put everything in a greased casserole and pour the tomato sauce over it. Put the Swiss cheese slices on top and bake it all in a 350 degree oven for about 15 to 20 minutes.

"When the cheese melts and gets all bubbly, you're ready."

TOM T. HALL'S CHOCOLATE CHESS PIE

¼ cup cocoa
1 tblsp. flour
1¼ cup sugar
1½ tblsp. corn meal
1½ tsp. vinegar

1 tsp. vanilla
2 eggs
½ cup melted margarine
¼ cup milk
1 unbaked pie shell

"First of all, mix the cocoa and the flour and the sugar and the corn meal together. And work all of the lumps out of the cocoa.

"Next, add the vinegar and vanilla. Then beat in the eggs, then the melted margarine, then the milk.

"When it's all put together, pour everything into an unbaked pie crust and bake for around 45 minutes at 325 degrees, or until it looks set and brown.

"Now you've got some serious pie eating to do."

ARLENE HARDEN'S ITALIAN SPAGHETTI

1 lb. hamburger
2 tblsp. chopped parsley
4 medium onions, chopped
4 cloves garlic, finely chopped
¼ cup butter
2 8 oz. cans tomato puree

2 6 oz. cans tomato paste
2 tsp. Worcestershire sauce
¼ cup olive oil
1 lb. spaghetti
Salt to taste
Parmesan cheese

"First, brown the hamburger. Then when you've drained it and set it aside, saute the parsley, onions and garlic in butter until they're soft.

"Add the tomato puree, tomato paste and Worcestershire sauce and stir in the browned hamburger. Then cook the sauce slowly — at least for three hours, and preferably longer.

"Add the olive oil to the water you cook the spaghetti in. When you serve it up, pour the sauce over the cooked, salted spaghetti, sprinkle on some Parmesan cheese and dig in.

"This recipe serves eight. It was used by my late brother-in-law, so it has sentimental value as well as being delicious."

ROY HEAD'S SPAGHETTI SAUCE

1 lb. lean hamburger
1 medium onion (chopped)
2 15 oz. cans tomato sauce
2 5½ oz. cans tomato juice
1 clove garlic (crushed)

¼ cup grated Parmesan cheese
1 tsp. sugar
1 cup or more fresh
   mushrooms (or canned)
Salt and pepper to taste

"Brown the hamburger and chopped onions, then add the tomato sauce, the tomato juice, and all the rest of the ingredients and bring everything to a boil.

"Then turn the heat down and let it simmer for about two hours.

"When you pour this sauce over your cooked spaghetti, sprinkle on a little more grated Parmesan cheese if you like.

"This recipe serves about six people. I got it from Mr. and Mrs. Lee Savaggio and it's since become one of my favorite dishes."

FERLIN HUSKY'S "CHILI EL FERLIN"

1 lb. precooked, diced chicken
(or diced shrimp or
diced lamb)
1 lb. precooked, diced pork
tenderloin (last night's pork
chops work fine)
1 lb. hamburger, browned
1 small or medium onion,
chopped
1 green pepper, chopped
4 fresh mushrooms

1 tsp. garlic powder (or 2 cloves
finely chopped garlic — I do
like garlic!)
1 cube butter or margarine
3 10 oz. cans of tomatoes and
green chilies (or 3 cans
mashed tomatoes)
2 or 3 16 oz. cans of chili beans
(or pinto beans)
1 large can of tomato juice
(more if desired)
4 tblsp. chili powder
Salt and pepper to taste

"**P**ut the precooked meats — the diced chicken and pork and browned hamburger — in a big pot. Then in a skillet, saute the chopped onion, green pepper, mushrooms and garlic in the butter and throw them in the pot, too.

"Next, add the tomatoes and green chilies, the chili beans and enough tomato juice to give you the thickness you want. Season with chili powder, salt and pepper.

"Bring it all to a boil, then let it simmer for an hour or longer — it depends on how hungry everyone is.

"This is an excellent dish for large or small groups of people, and it's good for using up leftover meat. If you have more guests than expected, stretch it by serving 'Chili El Ferlin' over noodles or rice."

THE KENDALLS' CHEDDAR POTATOES

6 slices bacon (fried and
    crumbled)
¼ lb. butter

1 cup grated cheddar cheese
2 lbs. sliced red potatoes,
    unpeeled

"**A**ll you do is parboil the sliced potatoes, layer all the ingredients in a casserole dish and bake it at 350 degrees for 45 minutes.

"But watch out — these spuds can be habit-forming."

DOUG KERSHAW'S CHICKEN & SAUSAGE GUMBO

1 cup Cajun roux (see below)
1 cut up hen or other fowl
1 lb. country sausage, cut into
    one inch pieces
1 bay leaf
2 large cloves of garlic, chopped

2 onions
4 green onion tails, chopped
2 tblsp. salt
1 tsp. cayenne pepper
1 tblsp. file' gumbo

"**W**hile you boil the chicken in a large (approximately six quart) pan, make the Cajun roux.

"Here's how. Heat a black iron skillet and put in a half cup of shortening. Let it get hot, but don't let it smoke. Sprinkle in a half cup of flour and stir until the mixture is even. Keep stirring until the roux is dark brown — it'll take about 15 minutes. If it starts to smoke, turn down the heat. But don't stop stirring until the roux is done.

"When the roux is ready, pour it into the pot with the chicken after you've skimmed the fat from the top of the pot. Then add all the rest of the ingredients except the file gumbo. Fill the pot with water and simmer for an hour and a half to two hours, until the chicken almost falls off the bone. Then add the file gumbo and serve immediately over cooked rice."

DICKEY LEE'S
FAVORITE RECIPE

LA WANDA LINDSEY'S SOUPER SUPPER CASSEROLE

1 lb. ground beef
1 can Cream of Mushroom soup
1 large onion, chopped
1 can (4 oz.) chopped green chilies

½ cup milk
1 dozen corn tortillas
1 lb. grated cheese

"Brown the ground beef and the onion together, then drain. Fry the tortillas lightly. Then combine the soup, milk and chilies.

"Next, line the bottom of a large casserole dish with half the tortillas. Follow with a layer of meat, then a layer of cheese, then a layer of soup. Repeat the layers, ending with soup on the top.

"Sprinkle cheese over the top layer and bake at 350 degrees for 30 to 40 minutes."

BOB LUMAN'S SAUTEED MUSHROOMS

*About 4 cups fresh mushrooms,
   washed*
1 tblsp. soy sauce

½ stick butter
1 small onion, chopped
½ tsp. lemon juice

"**C**ombine everything in a covered frying pan and bring to a boil on medium heat.

"Then remove the lid and simmer gently until the liquid thickens somewhat. This takes about half an hour.

"You can add more soy sauce if you like your mushrooms a bit saltier.

"Spoon a little of the mushroom gravy over meat. Mmmm — good!"

JODY MILLER'S DRESSING

2 cups of unfresh bread
2 cups of unfresh cornbread
1 small onion, chopped
½ cup butter

4 eggs, beaten
½ cup chopped celery
Chicken or turkey broth
Sage, salt and pepper to taste

"**C**rumble up the bread and cornbread and mix it all up with the chopped onion, celery, butter and spices. Then let it set a while.

"If you have broth from a chicken or a turkey to mix in, that's super. But if not, get some cans of chicken or turkey broth and stir it in along with the four eggs. Add broth until the consistency is right.

"My grandma used to taste it before adding the broth. I don't do this. I never taste food I'm preparing before I serve it — the thought is repulsive."

RONNIE MILSAP'S "MOONSHINE"

10 apples, *quartered*
2 packages carrots

1 stalk celery

"For this recipe you need a juice extractor, like a Vita Mix.

"You wash and quarter the apples, but don't peel them. You clean the celery. And you wash and scrape the carrots, removing the tops.

"The juice extractor does the rest — just combine all the ingredients in the machine, one at a time, and you have a delicious 'pick-me-up' that's good and natural."

MISTY MORGAN'S (AND JACK BLANCHARD'S) RICH CHEESECAKE

1½ cups crushed graham crackers
1½ cups sugar
1 tsp. cinnamon
⅛ tsp. salt
1 tblsp. lemon juice
1 tsp. vanilla

1/3 cup butter
2 cups sour cream
4 eggs
2 lbs. cream cheese
1 can cherry pie filling

"**M**ix the crushed graham crackers with a quarter cup of the sugar plus the cinnamon and the butter, and press it into a pan.

"Beat the eggs with a cup of sugar until they're thick and yellow. Then melt the cream cheese, preferably in a double boiler so it won't burn, and add the egg mixture with the lemon juice and salt and beat well. Pour it all into your crumb-lined pan, bake it at 375 degrees for half an hour, and take it out of the oven.

"Next, mix the sour cream, a quarter cup of sugar and the vanilla together and spread it on top of the cake. Return it to the oven for ten minutes at 475 degrees.

"After the cheesecake cools at room temperature for three hours, spread the cherry pie filling over the top and serve. Mmmmmm.

"This is a favorite for both Jack and me. I make these cakes for friends at Christmas time — as many as ten in one day — and everyone likes it as they usually get fruit cake every year."

ANNE MURRAY'S PORK PIE TOURTIERES

1 lb. ground beef
1 lb. ground pork
1 small onion, chopped
1 clove garlic
1 tsp. cloves
1 tsp. cinnamon

1 tsp. salt
¼ tsp. pepper
½ cup boiling water
Pastry for two 9 inch double-crust
    pie shells

"Combine the meat, onion, garlic and spices in a big heavy frying pan, like the cast iron kind. Add the boiling water and cook slowly until the meat loses its pink color, stirring constantly.

"Then spread the meat into two uncooked pie shells and top with pie dough. Seal the edges and puncture the crust. And don't forget to brush the top crust with cream.

"Bake in a hot oven — about 450 degrees — for half an hour. Then serve piping hot.

"You'll find these pies have even more flavor when you reheat them later."

JIMMY C. NEWMAN'S CAJUN VEGETABLE SOUP

1½ lbs. beef brisket
1½ lb. soup bone
½ head of cabbage, cut or diced
1 can whole tomatoes
1 cup diced potatoes
½ cup diced turnips
½ cup corn

1 cup frozen string beans
1 cup minced onion
1 cup diced celery
1 cup diced carrots
3 quarts water
½ cup vermicilli

"**S**alt the water to taste and bring it to a boil with the brisket and the soup bone. Let it boil for one hour. Then add the vegetables.

"Cook until the meat and vegetables are tender. You can add additional water to maintain the amount wanted.

"Throw in the vermicilli for the last 15 minutes of cooking. Then season to taste with salt and pepper."

STELLA PARTON'S MISSISSIPPI MUD CAKE

2 cups sugar
1/3 cup cocoa
2 sticks butter (or margarine)
1½ cups plain flour
1 tsp. baking powder
1 cup walnuts or pecans
1 cup coconut
4 eggs
1 jar of marshmallow cream

Frosting:
1 box powdered sugar
1/3 cup cocoa
1 stick butter (or margarine)
5 tblsps. milk or cream
1 tsp. vanilla flavoring

"Mix the first seven ingredients together. Then add the four eggs, one at a time.

"Cook in a large pan at 350 degrees for 30 minutes.

"After the cake is removed from the oven and has cooled, spread a jar of marshmallow cream on top of it and frost."

JEANNE PRUETT'S ICED TEA

5 Lipton tea bags   1 cup sugar
1½ cups water

"**B**ring the water to a hard boil. Add 5 teabags, *cover* and remove from heat quickly. Let the tea steep for a full 30 minutes.

"Then measure ten cups of cool water into a pitcher, add the cup of sugar and stir vigorously.

"Pour the concentrated tea *into* the water and mix well. This process is simple, but it's so important for making really good iced tea!"

BOBBY G. RICE'S APPLE SQUARES

2 cups flour
¾ cup shortening
½ tsp. salt
½ tsp. baking powder
1 egg, beaten

7 tbslp. water
A bunch of apples, peeled
    and cut up
Sugar and cinnamon to taste
Powdered sugar frosting

"**M**ix the flour, shortening, salt and baking powder together like pie dough. And also mix in the beaten egg and the water.

"Then divide the dough into halves. Roll out the first half, put it on a cookie sheet and pile on the apples, sugar and cinnamon, like you would to make a pie. Then roll out the rest of the dough and put it over the apples, pinching the top and bottom layers together all the way around so it's sealed.

"Now bake it for 40 minutes at about 400 degrees. When it's done, frost with a thin powdered sugar frosting and eat it while it's warm!"

CHARLIE RICH'S PUMPKIN BREAD

1½ cup sugar
½ cup cooking oil
2 eggs
1 cup pumpkin
1¾ cup flour
¼ tsp. baking powder
1 tsp. soda
1 tsp. salt

½ tsp. cloves
½ tsp. cinnamon
½ tsp. nutmeg
½ tsp. allspice
1/3 cup water
½ cup raisins, dates, currants
   or nuts

"Mix the sugar and oil. Add the eggs, then the pumpkin.

"Sift the dry ingredients together and add to the mixture. Then add the water.

"Bake at 350 degrees for 45 minutes to an hour, and that's it.

"My mother made this bread when I was little, and now my wife Margaret Ann has the recipe."

JEANNIE SEELY'S HAM TRIPLE WINNER

"I guess once you've been poor you never get out of the habit of making the most of a good thing. Here's a 'triple winner' that we do here at the farm quite often.

"We start with a good uncooked ham which we bake all day, and it serves as the base of any good meal.

"But the second time around, we take the ham bone with whatever meat is left on it, which is usually considerable, and make a ham boiled dinner. That consists of adding potatoes, carrots, celery, cabbage and spices to your imagination and taste.

"Then, for the third time around with this same ham bone and bits of meat, we make my special favorite — Navy Bean Soup. This consists of everything left over from the boiled dinner, and of course the navy beans. Plus we add finely chopped onion, more celery (leaves and all) and lots of grated carrots.

"Seasoning is again according to your taste, and I'll guarantee it'll smell so good that if any one should stop by while it's cooking you'll have some extra dinner guests!"

T. G. SHEPPARD'S CREAMED SWEET POTATOES

6 medium sweet potatoes	*Caramel sauce:*
1 stick butter	1 stick butter
1¼ cups sugar	1 cup sugar
A dash of nutmeg (optional)	½ cup cream
1 tsp. salt	1 tsp. vanilla

"**W**ash and boil the sweet pototoes in their jackets until they're tender. Then peel and rinse them, season with the remaining ingredients and whip everything together until it's all fluffy.

"The caramel sauce is made by melting the butter in a skillet, adding the sugar and letting it brown slowly over low heat, stirring until the desired color is obtained. Add the cream and the vanilla and boil the sauce for two minutes.

"To serve, you just pour the sauce over the potatoes and add some pecans if you want.

"This is a favorite recipe at holiday and Sheppard family gatherings."

RED SOVINE'S UPSIDE DOWN MEATLOAF

1 egg, beaten	2 cups bread crumbs
¾ cup milk	1 onion, minced
1 tsp. poultry seasoning	2 lbs. ground beef
1½ tsp. salt	5 or 6 strips bacon
A dash of pepper	

"Set your oven for 350 degrees and combine the first six ingredients. Then let them stand for about 5 minutes and add the onion and the meat.

"Mix everything up real well. Then line a loaf pan with the bacon strips and pack the mixture into the pan.

"After you bake it for an hour and a half at 350 degrees, take the meatloaf out of the oven and turn it over on a baking sheet, lifting off the pan. Raise the oven temperature to 450 degrees. Then put the meatloaf back in for another ten minutes, or until the bacon's crisp.

"This recipe makes about eight servings, or for real meatloaf lovers about six."

THE STATLER BROTHERS' MOUNTAIN POUND CAKE

½ lb. butter (2 sticks)
½ cup Crisco (Crisco only)
3 cups sugar
5 eggs
3 cups flour

1 cup milk
½ tsp. baking powder
1½ tsp. vanilla
½ tsp. lemon juice (optional)

"Cream the butter, Crisco and sugar and mix in the eggs one at a time. Then stir in your flour and milk alternately. Add the baking powder with the last of the flour. Add the flavorings last.

"Pour it all into a greased and floured 10 inch tube pan and place it in a cold oven. Set the oven to 350 degrees and bake for an hour and 15 minutes.

"Don't open the oven door — even once!

"When it's done, take the cake out of the oven and let it stand on a rack and cool completely before you take it out of the pan.

"This recipe comes from Harold Reid's family. We always have some along on the bus when we go on tour."

NAT STUCKEY'S SHRIMP CASSEROLE

1 lb. shelled uncooked shrimp
1 can condensed Cream of
  Mushroom soup
3 cups cooked brown rice
  (or white)
¾ cup diced cheddar cheese

1 tblsp. chopped green pepper
2 tblsp. lemon juice
2 tblsp. Worcestershire sauce
2 tblsp. melted butter
A dash of parsley, caraway seeds,
  celery seeds, salt and pepper

"This is my mother-in-law's recipe — Frankie Monkhouse — and it's one of my favorites.

"You just mix all the ingredients together and pour it into a buttered three quart casserole dish. Then you bake it for an hour at 375 degrees.

"Serve it with a nice salad and some corn chips. It's filling, and it tastes great."

HANK THOMPSON'S DEER CHILI

5 lbs. venison, chunked
(not ground)
1 lb. ground pork
1 small tub of margarine
Several cloves of garlic,
chopped
2 medium onions, chopped
2 cans stewed tomatoes, (home
canned are even better)
1 can tomatoes and green chilies
1 can mexicorn (optional)

Chili blend (Morton's preferred;
use as directed on package)
1 tsp. cumin
A few shakes or more of crushed
red pepper
1 tblsp. shaved _unsweetened_
chocolate
10 to 12 shakes of Worcestershire
sauce
1 tblsp. Adolph's tenderizer
or MSG
Salt and pepper

"**P**ut your meat, margarine, garlic, onions, Worcestershire sauce, tenderizer and salt and pepper in a large pot — cast iron is preferred — and brown lightly.

"Add the tomatoes, tomatoes and chilies and chili blend, and cook slowly for a couple of hours. Then add the cumin, mexicorn, chocolate and red pepper and simmer everything for another half hour. If you can let it stand overnight, it'll taste even better.

"While preparing the chili, it is important to drink two or three beers or a couple of large glasses of your favorite wine.

"Good eatin'."

ERNEST TUBB'S CHILI

2 lbs. coarsely ground or
  chopped beef
½ cup tallow drippings or lard
½ cup chopped onions
2 tblsp. minced garlic
4 tblsp. chili powder
2 tblsp. paprika

½ tsp. red pepper
1 tsp. salt (more if desired)
Juice of one lemon
3 4 oz. cans tomato sauce
1 cup of water and flour paste,
  cooked brown

"**B**rown the meat, add all the rest of the ingredients and cook slowly for one hour, adding water as needed. Then serve it over beans or rice.

"It's hard to grow up in Texas and not learn how to make good chili. I inherited this recipe from my dad, C. R. Tubb, Sr."

JACKY WARD'S TEXAS SHISH KA BOB

*Rib Eye steaks (about 8 oz.
    per person)*
Onions
Cayenne pepper to taste

Sauce:
1 15 oz. can tomato sauce
½ cup catsup
¼ cup Heinz 57 sauce
¼ cup Worcestershire sauce
1 tblsp. dried mustard

1 tblsp. sugar
*2 tblsp. lemon juice (or ½ lemon
    squeezed*
*1 clove garlic (or 1 tblsp.
    garlic salt)*
*½ chopped onion (or 1 tblsp.
    onion salt)*
2 tblsp. A1 steak sauce
1 strip bacon, quartered
*Texas or Louisiana Hot Sauce
    to taste*

"Cut the steak into healthy chunks and slide them onto skewers alternating with chunks of onion.

"Heat some cooking oil in a deep skillet to the boiling point. Then cook the shish ka bob in the hot oil for 30 seconds to a minute. When you take them out, sprinkle them generously with cayenne pepper (for children you may want to skip this step). And serve covered with a whole lot of sauce.

"To make the sauce, you just cook all the ingredients in a saucepan over medium heat for about 20 minutes."

DOC WATSON'S BLUEBERRY PIE

4 cups of fresh blueberries
1 can sweetened condensed milk
Juice of 2 large lemons

1 large carton of Cool Whip
2 9-inch baked pie shells

"Get the blueberries all washed and drained. Then blend the milk, lemon juice and Cool Whip together.

"Stir in the blueberries and pour it all into two pie crusts and chill.

"It's pretty simple, but just wait till you try it."

DON WILLIAMS' PECAN PIE

3 eggs
¾ cup sugar
1 cup Karo syrup (dark or light)
Dash of salt

1 tsp. vanilla
1 cup of whole pecan halves
2 or 3 pats of butter
1 9 inch unbaked pie shell

"Beat the eggs, and mix them well with the sugar, syrup, salt and vanilla.

"Pour the pecans into an unbaked pie shell. And on top of them, put two or three pats of butter.

"Then pour the mixture over the pecans and bake for an hour at 375 degrees.

"This is one of the first pies my wife Joy ever made for me. It might help explain why we've been married so long."

HANK WILLIAMS, JR.'S GROUND BEEF CASSEROLE

1½ lb. ground beef
1 cup tomato sauce
1 cup tomato paste
1 onion, chopped
1 bell pepper, chopped

8 oz. cottage cheese
½ cup mayonnaise
1 package medium sized noodles
Salt and pepper to taste

"While you cook the noodles in salt water, brown the ground beef in a bit of butter and season it with salt and pepper.

"Add the tomato paste and tomato sauce to the ground beef and stir it in. But mix the onion, bell pepper, mayonnaise and cottage cheese together separately.

"Then, combine everything and put it in a greased casserole dish. Cook it for 45 minutes or so at 350 degrees, and dinner is served."

INDEX

MAIN DISHES (CONT.)

SALADS

ABOUT THE AUTHOR

R. Moland Reynolds

Tom Wiecks was once the highest-paid American disc jockey in Iceland. (Which isn't saying much — as a Navy E-5, he ran the American Forces Radio station on the NATO base in Keflavik, staffed by E-4's, 3s and 2s.

Since then, he's worked for KUIK, KJIB and KWJJ in Portland. But mostly he's been writing ads — "everything from matchbook covers to skywriting" — including some radio and tv commercials that have won national and international awards.

He and his wife Carolyn live in West Linn, Oregon. They have two children, Sarah, almost 5, and Jamie, 1, plus an ornery black cat named Obie. The last two bite people.

SEND ME "THE BEST COOKIN' IN THE COUNTRY"

□ Enclosed is my check for _____ book(s) @ $6.95
($5.95 plus $1.00 postage and handling).

□ Please charge my VISA or MC account. My card
_____ Expires _____

Mail to:
Barleycorn Books
290 SW Tualatin Loop
West Linn, Oregon 97068

My name _____

My address _____

City _____

State _____ Zip _____

- -

SEND ME "THE BEST COOKIN' IN THE COUNTRY"

□ Enclosed is my check for _____ book(s) @ $6.95
($5.95 plus $1.00 postage and handling).

□ Please charge my VISA or MC account. My card
_____ Expires _____

Mail to:
Barleycorn Books
290 SW Tualatin Loop
West Linn, Oregon 97068

My name _____

My address _____

City _____

State _____ Zip _____

- -

SEND ME "THE BEST COOKIN' IN THE COUNTRY"

□ Enclosed is my check for _____ book(s) @ $6.95
($5.95 plus $1.00 postage and handling).

□ Please charge my VISA or MC account. My card
_____ Expires _____

Mail to:
Barleycorn Books
290 SW Tualatin Loop
West Linn, Oregon 97068

My name _____

My address _____

City _____

State _____ Zip _____

- -

SEND ME "THE BEST COOKIN' IN THE COUNTRY"

□ Enclosed is my check for _____ book(s) @ $6.95
($5.95 plus $1.00 postage and handling).

□ Please charge my VISA or MC account. My card
_____ Expires _____

Mail to:
Barleycorn Books
290 SW Tualatin Loop
West Linn, Oregon 97068

My name _____

My address _____

City _____

State _____ Zip _____